Name:

_____

Alias (fake name you use when you need to get out of trouble):

_____

Super-alias (fake name for when your regular alias is already in too much trouble):

_____

Name of the person who should read this journal in case you accidentally get thrown back in time but left clues for how you can be returned to the present:

_____

Name you would give to a sword that glows whenever a teacher is about to give you a pop quiz:

_____

Name you would give to a guinea pig who is also a wizard:

_____

Favorite topping for toast:

_____

To my pigs, the best people I know
—JB

BuzzPop
an imprint of Little Bee Books

251 Park Avenue South, New York, NY 10010 | Text copyright © 2020 by James Breakwell
Illustrations and photos by James Breakwell | Author photograph by Van Deman Photography
Cover design by Lisa Vega | Additional image credits: Cover and title page, cute unicorn
(© by Yurlick), cloud designed by starline/Freepik, page 8, messy bedroom, designed by
vectorpouch/Freepik, pages 9, 11, 46, 56, 57, 62, 63, and 64, Unicorn Patch (© by Chinch),
page 65, minivan (© by Photoroyalty/Freepik), page 71, of the unicorn, (© by Edward Topsell),
page 74, Zombies (© by Zdenek Sasek), interior sketch (© by SVEG)
Manufactured in China TPL 0320 | First Edition

1 3 5 7 9 10 8 6 4 2

ISBN 978-1-4998-1031-8

buzzpopbooks.com

For information about special discounts on bulk purchases, please
contact Little Bee Books at sales@littlebeebooks.com.

James Breakwell

PRANCE LIKE NO ONE'S WATCHING

A GUIDED JOURNAL FOR EXPLODING UNICORNS

BuzzPop

How to Journal

Start at the beginning
and stop at the end. Go bonkers in
the middle.

Foreword 1

You're Funny. Yes, YOU. 3

My Kind of Kids 4

Hidden Humor 10

The Art of the Joke 14

You, Meet You 28

Laugh It Off 33

Kidding with Kids 44

Animated Animals 49

Home Is Where the Punch Line Is 54

Chuckle, Don't Choke 57

Cracked Up by the Bell 61

What a Trip 63

Art Attack 67

Unicorns Have a Point 70

Zombie Dodging 73

Today's Setups, Tomorrow's Punch Lines 82

Congratulations, Comedy Ninja 87

Answer Key 89

A Short Goodbye 90

Foreword

My name is **James Breakwell**, and I've been finding the humor around me for years, even when the only person I've amused was me. I'm surrounded by sources of laughter. I have four daughters, ages nine and under; one wife, age don't ask; and two pigs, ages don't matter because pigs are timeless. I also have a dog, but I don't talk about him much because he's shy (and won't sign a release form). I write jokes about our lives together and post them on the Internet, where more than a million people read them. I also make web comics, create videos, write books, and in general, do anything I can to avoid actual work. So far, so good.

My life isn't any funnier than anyone else's. I just share the best parts of it to make the world a more interesting place. You can, too. I mean, you can share moments from your own life. If you shared moments from my life, that would be weird. In the coming pages, I'll help you find the humor that surrounds you at school, at home, and at the end of the world when undead monsters walk the earth. And if there's time, I'll also teach you how to fly. But there probably won't be time. It's been a busy Thursday.

You're funny. Yes, YOU.

And I don't mean funny-looking or funny as in odd. (Although you could be those things, too. I'm not here to judge.) No, I mean you have a great sense of humor. It's time to use it to its full potential because you're too awesome to be bored. This book will teach you how to find (and create!) amusement in the world around you using your naturally great sense of humor. And also how to tell the difference between a Pegasus and a unicorn, and how to color in an overly friendly cactus, and how to survive a zombie apocalypse. But mostly the humor thing. I might have bitten off more than I can chew.

My Kind of Kids

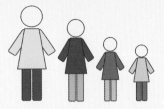

I love writing jokes about my kids. Let me tell you a little more about them so you'll understand why.

Kid: Betsy

Age: Oldest

Height: Tall enough to reach the cupboard where I hide my secret candy stash

Sworn enemy: Anyone who messes up her bed

Superpower: Getting the remote to work

Kid: Mae

Age: Oldest middle child

Height: Objects in rearview mirror are closer than they appear

Sworn enemy: Chicken tacos

Superpower: Speeding up or slowing down time depending on if she wants to be early or late

Kid: Lucy

Age: Youngest middle child

Height: About yea tall

Sworn enemy: Bedtime

Superpower: Big, innocent eyes that make adults bend to her will

Kid: Waffle (The internet picked that nickname)

Age: Timeless spirit of chaos

Height: Big enough to fill your nightmares

Sworn enemy: Order

Superpower: Destruction incarnate

Oh, and there's one other person you should know about.

Kid: Me (James, aka the Exploding Unicorn)

Age: Old enough to know better, or 34

Height: Tall enough to reach the top of the fridge

Sworn enemy: On good days, no one, on bad days, my kids Kidding.

Superpower: Laser eyes, levitation, lying about my superpowers

Fill out the same information for yourself:

*insert a picture of yourself here

Age: _____

Height: _____

Sworn enemy: _____

Superpower: _____

Take this quiz to find out which of my kids you're most like.

If I told you to pick up your room, what would you do?

Ⓐ Clean up the room but with a witty reply.

Ⓑ Not clean up the room but with a witty reply.

Ⓒ Completely ignore me and keep living your life.

Ⓓ Tear through the room like a tornado, leaving a trail of devastation in your wake.

If there was one piece of candy left and you and another person both wanted it, what would you do?

Ⓐ Share it.

Ⓑ Eat it yourself, but act like it was never there.

Ⓒ Eat it yourself without shame or denial because hunger justifies all.

Ⓓ Rummage through the fridge and eat everything else while the other person was distracted.

There's a zombie outside. What do you do?

Ⓐ Fight it.

Ⓑ Say you're going to fight it, but make sure someone else goes out the door first.

Ⓒ Don't say you're going to fight it, but watch as everyone else fights it for you.

Ⓓ Keep watching TV.

It's costume time. Which princess costume do you wear?

Ⓐ Mulan, because she's a great warrior.

Ⓑ Snow White, because mice and birds do her cleaning for her.

Ⓒ Tiana, because she can eat all she wants at her restaurant.

Ⓓ Sleeping Beauty, because you can fall asleep almost instantly in awkward places and you're really hard to wake up.

Which kid are you?

If you answered mostly A, you're Betsy. You're responsible, fierce, and dangerously witty.

If you answered mostly B, you're Mae. You're cunning, funny, and always looking for an angle to come out ahead.

If you answered mostly C, you're Lucy. You know what you want in life and you go for it. Woe to anyone who stands in your way.

If you answered mostly D, you're Waffle. You are an unstoppable force of nature. You are as mysterious as you are dangerous.

I told my kids to clean their room approximately 10,000 times. This took them all day. Can you tell what they cleaned up?

Circle the differences below.

Hint: It wasn't much.

Here are some posts I wrote about my kids.

Fill in the blanks to create your own punch lines.

> **5-year-old:** *holds out an empty plate* I need more ketchup.
> **Me:** You don't have any French fries.
> **5:** They get in the way.

> **Me:** Time for bed.
> **5-year-old:** I can't sleep. I'm an owl.
> **Me:** Fine. Go eat mice all night.
> **5:** _____

> **5-year-old:** *gallops into the room with a cowboy hat and a lightsaber*
> **Me:** Who are you?
> **5:** _____
> **Me:** Uh-oh.

Write a conversation of your own. Feel free to use my kids as characters.

Make yourself a little icon while you're at it.

> _____
> _____
> _____

Do you and your friends sound like my kids? I'm not sure if that's a good or bad thing.

9

Hidden Humor

Not everything you laugh about starts out funny. Sometimes it's just weird. Or annoying. Or completely mundane. What makes it funny is the way you look at it, either in the moment or in hindsight. Humor isn't an event; it's an attitude. I'd write that on my arm in permanent marker, but I'm afraid of that much commitment. So I'll just print it here.

What's something you couldn't laugh about at the time but can laugh about now when you look back on it?

_____

_____

_____

What's something that you can't laugh about now but you hope you can someday?

_____

_____

_____

_____

Who would win in a fight between a gorilla and a robot?

_____

_____

_____

_____

_____

Sorry, not related to the topic. I just need you to settle a bet.

Here are three things I couldn't laugh about at the time but did later, when I turned them into posts.

What it means when my 4-year-old flushes the toilet:

1 flush: Everything is fine.

2 flushes: Time to check the bathroom.

3 flushes: Time to call a plumber.

4 flushes: Time to move.

I spent an hour in the middle of the night trying to pry used gum out of my pig's mouth, so, yes, my life turned out exactly like I expected.

I had a big stain on my shirt. Someone asked if I was in a food fight. Yeah, with myself. I need to learn to use a napkin.

Write some posts about "disasters" in your own life, imaginary or real.

11

What was a time when you had a perfect joke but you didn't say it because you were too shy or thought of it a moment too late?

_____

_____

_____

What would have happened if you did say it?

_____

Are you happy you didn't, or do you wish you had?

_____

Let's say you earned a spot in the CLASS CLOWN HALL OF FAME. Write a few lines from your acceptance speech. Feel free to thank me.

Go you!

_____

_____

_____

_____

_____

_____

_____

_____

_____

Humor is truly personal. Something that makes you laugh *I should know. When I tell jokes in real life, I get nothing but eye rolls.* hysterically might make other people roll their eyes. But no worries. As long as you amuse yourself, you're doing it right.

What are three things you think are funny that someone else might not?

1. _____
   _____
   _____
   _____

2. _____
   _____
   _____
   _____

3. _____
   _____
   _____
   _____

I think those are funny, too. Or at least I would if I could read what you wrote, which I can't because you write too small. Maybe you should work on that.

If you can't laugh in the moment, you can laugh after the fact. What doesn't kill you makes you stronger. *Or at least gives you a good story to tell at parties.*

The Art of the Joke

There's no such thing as being in the wrong mood for jokes. I'll prove it.

- **Angry?** Jokes will help you calm down.
- **Sad?** Jokes will cheer you up.
- **Happy?** Jokes will spread your good mood.
- **Irritated?** Annoyances will give you material for new jokes.
- **Shy?** Jokes will break the ice.
- **Hungry?** Jokes will distract people while you steal their snacks.

Write the benefits of jokes when you're feeling:

Jealous _____

_____

Nervous _____

_____

Excited _____

_____

Purple _____

_____

Ambidextrous _____

Both left- and right-handed.

_____

Jokes have power. Use that power for good. Joke about funny situations, silly ideas, and of course, exploding unicorns.

Unicorns feel fine when they explode. They get better in no time.

Use jokes to make people happy. Remember, everyone is amazing, including you. And me. Especially me.

If you ever forget that you're amazing, do this word search. All of these words describe you. *Okay, maybe all but one or two.*

AWESOME	ORIGINAL	TRANSLUCENT
SMART	WEREWOLF	FLAMMABLE
FUNNY	UNDEAD	MADE OF GRAPES

```
S I E N Y A H R W Y H F A V S O X T S C
F G J N Y L H E H O R T V E H R V K T F
D L N S H I R S M Y T Q P H V I R Q H C
Z U A J K E Z W O P L A U B J G R U F R
F O U M W O B L I R R V C P H I U B P U
D X C O M P T N Z G U V R O G N Z O Y H
V A L N Z A R F F Y F N E U T A D C Z T
M F E G B J B O S N M T Y D B L E T W R
T O D D F M E L O C V J N G K A Z Y H A
K A P A N D G J E M O S E W A B Q X F M
J I Z S A U Z N Q L V X X K X D J Y Z S
H A A M T X L C Z T R A N S L U C E N T
```

15

Often the first thing that pops into your head is also the funniest.

Imagine yourself in each of these scenarios and write down the first thing you would blurt out.

Your friend walks into your classroom dressed as a clown.

You realize your friend is sitting right next to you and the clown is their evil clown doppelgänger.

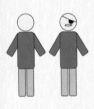

You realize everyone has an evil clown doppelgänger. You're in Evil Clown Doppelgänger World.

You realize you forgot your lunch on the bus.

Laughter makes memories.

When's the last time you laughed so hard you cried?

So hard milk came out your nose?

So hard you couldn't breathe?

So hard you slipped into another dimension for a few seconds? *Maybe don't do that again.*

Some things are always funny, no matter how many times you hear them.

What's an inside joke that always makes you and your friends crack up?

_____

_____

_____

_____

What's a movie that always makes you laugh, even if you've memorized all the jokes?

_____

What's a book that always makes you smile, even if you've read it so much the pages are falling out?

_____

What's an animal that makes you laugh based solely on how it looks?

_____

Write an apology to that animal.

_____

_____

_____

_____

_____

You can't laugh at someone's joke until you understand where they're coming from. Let's try on some other points of view to see what's funny. And what's not. Don't look at me like that.

If you had to spend a day in someone else's shoes, whose shoes would you steal?

_____

How do you get away with the shoes if you really love them, but their original owner still wants them back?

_____

_____

_____

What would you do if you could spend a day as a spider?

_____

_____

_____

As a pig? _____

_____

_____

_____

As a zombie? _____

_____

_____

_____

As me? _____

_____

_____

As you? (You might have some experience at this one.)

_____

_____

_____

You don't have to tell jokes in a comedy club. Here are some places you can test out your sense of humor:

- Text messages
- Notes to friends
- ~~Writing on a bathroom stall~~ *Don't do this. The janitor will not like it.*
- Shouting out a car window
- Surrounded by zombies and fighting for your life
- Sitting in your favorite chair petting a pig (or two)

What other places can you think of?

_____

_____

_____

_____

_____

_____

The only person you have
to make laugh is yourself.

Draw the ideal audience for your unique sense of humor.
It could be an auditorium full of people, a few close
friends, or even just yourself. *That last one is my favorite. I never disappoin*
my biggest fan.

Sometimes the best jokes get groans instead of laughs. *This is the humor that puts the "pun" in "Punishment."*

- **What do you call a male cow who can't stay awake?**
  A bulldozer.
- **What kind of dog is the best at finding a missing wedding ring?** A golden retriever.
- **What was wrong with the dairy farmer's jokes?**
  They were too cheesy.
- **Where do most spider couples first meet?** The web.
- **What do poker players fear at the beach?**
  Card sharks.

Don't let me have all the fun (and shame). Write some puns of your own.

Combine the adjectives on the left with the nouns on the right to create something original and funny, and write them below.

Weird Adjectives	**Weirder Nouns**
· Ninja	· Nun
· Glowing	· Outhouse
· Space	· Orangutan
· Waterlogged	· Puppy
· Super-buff	· Tomato
· Flying	· Bus
· Delicious	· Continent
· Singing	· Mongoose

Draw your favorite combination.

Not everything that makes you laugh is in the world around you. Sometimes it's in your head. I'd prove it, but I can't see inside your cranium, so here are some of the weirdest thoughts from inside mine.

Color them in and draw some of your own.

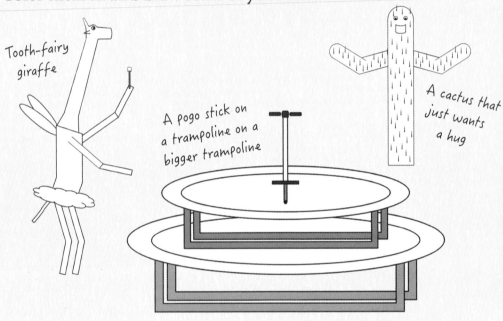

Tooth-fairy giraffe

A pogo stick on a trampoline on a bigger trampoline

A cactus that just wants a hug

The great thing about the internet is you can tell any kind of joke you want. I once made a social media account dedicated to writing haiku poems about breakfast foods. It didn't last very long, not because I ran out of material, but because it made me too hungry.

I ate some burned toast.
It tasted like smoke and ash.
More margarine please.

A haiku has 5 syllables in the first line, 7 in the next, and 5 in the last. They're usually about enjoying nature, but you can't eat that for breakfast.

Write your own breakfast haikus below.

_____

_____

_____

_____

_____

_____

_____

_____

I prefer writing jokes instead of saying them out loud. That way I don't have to worry about getting nervous or messing up my lines. *Except for typos. Social media doesn't always have an edit button.*

Do you prefer to tell jokes in front of other people or to write them down to share them? Or do you keep them to yourself in a guided journal like this one?

Take this quiz to find out which approach suits your personality the best.

When you stand in front of people, what do you do?
- Ⓐ Feel alive
- Ⓑ Actually become alive because you're a zombie who comes back from the dead
- Ⓒ Freeze (metaphorically)
- Ⓓ Freeze (literally—maybe you're Elsa)

Which sound do you like the most?
- Ⓐ Other people's laughter
- Ⓑ The clicking of your fingers on a keyboard
- Ⓒ Whatever you're blasting through your headphones
- Ⓓ Silence

When do you like to receive praise or compliments?
- Ⓐ Immediately
- Ⓑ After an awkward pause
- Ⓒ Eventually
- Ⓓ Never

Which of these is your best asset?
- Ⓐ Your funny voices
- Ⓑ Your timing
- Ⓒ Your typing
- Ⓓ Your grammar

If you answered mostly A or B, you prefer the excitement of telling jokes face-to-face. Congratulations, you're fun and outgoing.

If you chose mostly C or D, you prefer to be funny on the screen or the written page. Be careful. You're in danger of growing up to be like me.

If your answers are evenly split between A's and B's for in-person jokes and C's and D's for written ones, you are a living contradiction. Not even you understand you. Good. Life is more interesting that way.

Use your finely honed joke-telling skills to amuse yourself and your friends. There's nothing better than a good turn of the phrase. Until you send yourself in endless circles. *Please don't barf.*

You, Meet You

Nobody knows you better than you. But maybe you don't know yourself as well as you think.

Answer these deep, probing questions you've probably never thought about before.

How many snakes is too many snakes?

How big of an alligator do you think you could safely wrestle?

How many bees would it take to convince you to never go outside again?

Which could you live without for longer, food or internet?

How many tries does it take you to plug in a USB cord the right way?

If it's less than three, you're officially a wizard.

You have a unique sense of humor because there's no one else just like you. What are some things that you could write about from your life that nobody else could?

What's something about you no one else knows?

_____

What's something everyone believes about you that's not true?

_____

What's something about you that would surprise your parents if you told them?

_____

Which TV game show do you think you'd be the most likely to win?

_____

Which TV game show would most likely cause you to humiliate yourself and bring permanent shame to your family?

_____

If you could bring one animal back from extinction, what would you pick?

_____

What would happen when that animal escaped?

And if movies have taught us anything, it definitely would.

_____

_____

_____

_____

_____

_____

I'll do almost anything for a laugh. Or free food. What motivates you?

_____

_____

What's the worst thing you could be bribed to do in exchange for a lifetime of free tacos?

_____

_____

What would you forgive someone for in exchange for pizza?

_____

_____

What's the longest you can hold your breath while laughing?

_____

_____

Have you ever tried to keep your eyes open while sneezing? If yes, did your eyeballs explode?

_____

Probably not, since you're reading this—but I've been wrong before.

_____

 How fast could you run if you were chased by a ghost?

_____

_____

How fast could you run if that ghost had a mustache?

_____

_____

You can tell a lot about a person by the things they surround themselves with.

What's something in your room right now that you're proud of?

_____

_____

What's something in your room you wish you could get rid of? Siblings you share a room with don't count. Okay, they totally do.

_____

_____

What would be the perfect view from your window?

_____

_____

If you could take a priceless object from any museum and put it in your room, what would it be?

_____

_____

If you had a magic charm that could permanently ban one thing from your room, what would it be? I recommend banning bears in tuxes. A well-dressed bear is ALWAYS up to something.

_____

_____

_____

_____

_____

_____

You're hilarious, but you're not the only one.

Who is someone in your life who always makes you laugh?

_____

What makes them so funny?

_____
_____
_____
_____
_____

What's something you've said to make them laugh?

_____
_____
_____
_____
_____

Have you challenged them to a duel to steal their humor powers for yourself?   *I hope not. That's not how comedy works.*

_____
_____
_____
_____

Did you learn something about yourself? Good. The worst person for you to keep a secret from is you.

Humor is a form of escape. Sometimes we all need to get away.
If people in my family could run away, here's where they'd go:

- **Betsy:** Hogwarts
- **Mae:** A long time ago in a galaxy far, far away
- **Lucy:** A candy factory *One that doesn't actively harm children to teach a lesson about morality.*
- **Waffle:** She'd stay home so she can play with all the "off-limits" toys her sisters left unguarded
- **Me:** Any place I can take a nap without my kids finding me
- **My pigs:** The fridge *(to eat food, not to be food)*
- **My wife:** No idea *(She's way smarter than me.)*

If you could pick up everything and go away right now, where would you go?

_____

_____

_____

Why?

_____

_____

_____

Who would you take with you? *If it's someplace cool, you better take me.*

_____

_____

_____

It's good to laugh about the things you're afraid of. Here are some things I fear:

- Birds
- Sounds in the middle of the night
- Upsetting my pigs

Here are things I don't fear:

- Failure (I can always try again. And again.) *(And again.) I fail a lot.*
- Sounding silly or foolish

What are you afraid of? *I know this is totally personal to you, but you should have birds on this list because no one should trust them.*

_____

_____

_____

_____

_____

_____

_____

What aren't you afraid of? *Birds better not be on this list.*

_____

_____

_____

_____

_____

_____

_____

You have stressful experiences every day. Don't think of them as setbacks. Think of them as setups for your next great laugh.

What's the worst, most stressful thing that happened to you this week?

_____

_____

_____

_____

_____

_____

Was there anything funny about it in the moment?

_____

Was there anything funny about it afterward?

_____

If yes, draw what you found funny. *Or just draw a penguin in a fancy hat.*

Nobody's perfect. Sometimes our funniest stories are about mistakes we (or somebody we're close to) make. Lucy once got stuck in the back of a chair while trying to steal pudding off the dining room table. I helped her get unstuck. *After taking lots of pictures, of course.*

What's a mistake you made that seemed like a huge deal at the time but you can laugh about today?

_____

_____

If you could go back in time to that day, what would you do differently?

_____

_____

How would that change things for the better (or worse)?

_____

_____

Would you still make that change if you knew altering the timeline would cause an unspeakable tragedy, like chocolate becoming illegal, but would also save you mild embarrassment? Why or why not?

_____

_____

_____

SAVE THIS PAGE FOR WHEN YOU HAVE A "BAD" DAY.

Sometimes it might seem like you're having a bad day, but that's only because you have the wrong perspective. Just answer the following questions.

Did a beached whale roll over you?

_____

Did you get bitten by a radioactive spider but instead of superpowers, you just got diarrhea?

_____

Did you accidentally drink a potion that turned you inside out but also gave you perfect toenails?

_____

If none of those things happened, it sounds like your day wasn't really so bad after all.

Write some more bad things that didn't happen.

_____

_____

_____

_____

_____

_____

_____

_____

Some of the worst moments have the best humor potential. Rewrite each of these unfortunate events so you can laugh about them to yourself. I'll go first.

I failed a test.
Lower numbers are better, like in golf, right?

I overslept.
I got surprise bonus sleep. Go me.

I didn't make the team. I just won a bunch of free time for the rest of the season.

My dog ate my homework.
I don't have to worry about feeding my dog tonight.

The teacher called me the wrong name.
The teacher doesn't know who I am. I can get away with anything.

Now you try. **My friend won't talk to me.**

My teacher doesn't like me.

My room is too small.

I found out my dad is a Dark Lord of the Sith.

An evil genie cursed me to a lifetime of bad breath.

A friend forgot my birthday.

My parents grounded me for something I didn't do.

The hot new toy of the holidays sells out.

My secret crush likes someone else.

I pricked my finger on a spinning wheel and fell asleep for 100 years.

I made a post about whether my favorite drink is called "pop" or "soda" and accidentally started a fight online.

All right, but what about zombies?

If you have the right attitude, you can find the positives in anything. Highlight the upside of the zombie apocalypse. *I'll start.*

You can't leave the house.

School is canceled.

The power is out.

Every day is like camping.

Your turn. **Zombies moan loudly.**

You're running low on canned vegetables.

Phones stop working.

The roads are blocked.

Sometimes the funniest moments in life come from simple misunderstandings. My 4-year-old thought bald eagles were "bald beagles."

Draw a bald beagle.

Life is full of challenges. Rank the challenges below in order from 1 to 11, with 1 being the easiest for you and 11 being the most difficult.

_____ Convincing your parents to let you stay up late

_____ Juggling chain saws that are running and on fire

_____ Convincing your teacher to give you extra credit

_____ Catching an electric eel with your bare hands

_____ Talking to your crush

_____ Fighting off a horde of zombies in a parking lot

_____ Finding a unicorn

_____ Getting three or more people to agree on what to do

_____ Brushing a dragon's teeth

_____ Being comfortable in your own skin

_____ Being comfortable in someone else's skin

Sometimes people push your buttons. Buttons are hard to resist. That's why elevators are so much fun. But people aren't elevators (at least not usually). Unless you're a parent. Then people ALWAYS push your buttons. *I'm looking at you, all four of my kids.*

Draw a line from these buttons to your reaction when someone pushes them. If these reactions don't describe you, write in your own.

Buttons

- Laughing at you

- Eating the last cookie

- Not believing in you

- Banishing you to the shadow realm

- Telling you it's over because they have the high ground

Reactions

- Ignoring them

- Taking a nap

- Making up a song-and-dance number on the spot

- Being nice

- Doing a backflip over them with your lightsaber drawn

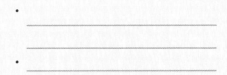

- _____
  _____

- _____
  _____

Now that you know what your buttons are, how do you plan to avoid getting them pressed? Me, I like to leave the area as quickly as possible. I'm not afraid to push my own EJECT button.

Kidding with Kids

As we get older, we get smarter. But sometimes the best wisdom comes from the very young.

Here are some helpful lessons from my kids:

- Your siblings are your best friends. And your worst enemies. Sometimes at the same time.
- Anything worth doing is worth whining about first.
- If at first you don't succeed, try it again 1,000 times while screaming, "I can do it myself!"
- Pens are good for drawing on paper but better for drawing on skin and best of all for drawing on walls.
- You'll never be lonely when you have a pig.

What are some lessons you learned when you were very young?

_____

_____

_____

_____

_____

_____

_____

_____

_____

Here are some life hacks from a toddler:

- You can't lose your stuff if you sleep with it all in your bed.
- Matching clothes are always optional.
- No two shoes should ever be in the same spot. Getting dressed should be a scavenger hunt.
- If I can't see you, you can't see me.
- It's okay to have dessert before a meal. And during the meal. And after a meal. In fact, just have dessert.
- Always say exactly what you think, even if you're hard to understand and don't know any big words.

Think like a toddler. What other life hacks might a toddler have?

_____
_____
_____
_____
_____
_____
_____
_____
_____
_____
_____
_____

Not everything gets easier with age. The older you get, the harder it is to make friends. But for younger kids, it's the easiest thing in the world.

4-year-old: *holds up teddy bear* He's my best friend.

Me: I thought I was your best friend.

4: He doesn't ask to share my snacks.

Me: *lives next door to someone for 10 years*
never asks their name

9-year-old: *met someone at the park 10 seconds ago*
already planned a joint trip to space

Do you find it easy or hard to make friends?

_____

What's something you could do to have more friends?

_____
_____
_____
_____

What's something you could do to have fewer friends? They can be a lot of work.

_____
_____
_____
_____

Dressed to thrill...

My daughters love dressing up like princesses and dueling with lightsabers. There's nothing that says you can't look fabulous while you fight evil, regardless of who you are.

Is there anything someone has told you that you can't enjoy because of your gender? Your age? Your size? Draw it below.

Now go live it out in real life. Unless it requires you to go into space or survive the zombie apocalypse or something. Then you might have to wait a while.

My kids each have their own unique sense of style. They're not afraid to mix and match Batman capes, Spider-Man masks, and princess gowns.

Which superhero or fictional character outfits would you combine to create your ultimate ensemble?

_____

_____

_____

_____

Where would you wear it?

_____

Draw it below.

Younger kids don't know much about the world, but they know exactly what they want. That's what makes them hilarious. And dangerous. *Keep a fire extinguisher handy just in case.*

Animated Animals

Everybody loves animals. They're funny and smart and weird all at the same time. They remind me of myself, but only the weird part.

My favorite animal is a pig. I have two: an adult pig named Gilly and a baby one named Luna. They both live in my house. In fact, they take turns sharing beds with my kids at night.

That's normal, right?

Here's why pigs rock:

- They never lie to you. They want food and they want companionship, in that order. You always know where you stand with them.
- Aside from their pellets and vegetables, they eat grass, so they keep the lawn in check. Now that I have two, I might never have to mow again.
- They're really strong. I don't want some flimsy animal my kids might break. Gilly is durable enough to withstand even the toughest toddler. Luna will get there soon.
- Pigs can't fly, but they can jump. Gilly loves to leap into my kids' beds.

It's cute as long as you're not under her when she lands.

Can you think of any reasons why your favorite kind of pet is cool?

If you can't, just write "because they are" and you'll be right.

_____

_____

_____

_____

_____

_____

_____

_____

My kids love animals, even if those animals aren't pigs. *Or real.*

Find these hard-to-find animals in this word search.

SASQUATCH	CHUPACABRA	LOCH NESS MONSTER	GLASS SHARK
YETI	VAMPIRE BAT	LASER PENGUIN	GHOST SLOTH

```
T A B E R I P M A V X K M X E S C S K J
E C F F R T A V T T K O K R E V H A R X
G L O P D J E Z K M W O Q F O D U S A L
R E T S N O M S S E N H C O L J P Q H R
I J H W Y H N N F U I N H U A T A U S X
K E I Y G G F U J P G P L F E W C A S P
B Z E N L A S E R P E N G U I N A T S S
R T I J W I I U O U T J M E F A B C A N
I F W F Z J D J W T W V W W O T R H L A
U D L B N N U X S X A I M Z V U A O G Q
G H O S T S L O T H P U S O V J K N A P
```

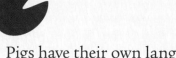

Pigs have their own language.

After listening to Gilly and Luna, I know the meaning of every sound they make. Here's a cheat sheet for what they're saying:

- **Oink:** I'm a pig.
- **Oink:** Still a pig.
- **Oink:** I smell food.
- **Oink:** I like you. You give me food.
- **Oink:** Why aren't you giving me food right now?
- **Oink:** Your bed is comfy. It belongs to me now.
- **Oink:** Seriously, what's the status on that food?
- **Oink:** I'm too good for mud. I'll stick with the air-conditioning.
- **Oink:** I love you. Okay, I tolerate you. Best you're going to get.

Is there a pet in your life? Write down what their noises mean.

_____

_____

_____

_____

_____

_____

_____

_____

_____

Take this quiz to find out
what animal you are.

If you saw a cake on the table, what would you do?
- Ⓐ Pull on the tablecloth to knock it to the floor, then eat the whole thing.
- Ⓑ Slice it with your magical horn.
- Ⓒ Wait for someone to pet you, then steal a piece off their plate.
- Ⓓ Use your two human hands to get a slice.

If your friend were feeling sad, what would you do?
- Ⓐ Keep eating.
- Ⓑ Cheer them up with your magical unicorn powers.
- Ⓒ Cheer them up by wagging your tail and being cute.
- Ⓓ Cheer them up by talking about their problems with human words using your human vocal cords.

Which of these foods would you never eat?
- Ⓐ Pork
- Ⓑ Unicorn burgers
- Ⓒ Hot dogs
- Ⓓ A fellow human

How would you prefer to stay cool?
- Ⓐ Roll in mud
- Ⓑ Prance through a breezy meadow
- Ⓒ Pant
- Ⓓ Turn on the air-conditioning

What animal are you?

If you answered mostly A, you're a pig, noblest of farm animals.

If you answered mostly B, you're a unicorn, noblest of the mythical creatures.

If you answered mostly C, you're a dog, noblest of household pets.

If you answered mostly D, you're a human, noblest of all Earth's creatures—except for dolphins, who can jump 15 feet in the air and do backflips. We can't compete with that.

Draw yourself riding a dolphin. *You'll have to catch it first.*

Animals are the best things in our lives. They can make us laugh, but almost never make us cry. Just don't replace all the people in your life with pets. You still need at least one adult who can drive you to the store for more pet food.

Home Is Where the Punch Line Is

Most of my family's adventures happen at home. Answer these questions about your own house. *Or don't.*
Do whatever you want. I'm not your mom.

If you could install a secret passageway anywhere in your house, where would you put it?

_____

If you close the door to your room, from how many rooms away can people hear you yodel?

_____

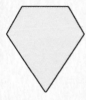

What's the best place in your house to hide a diamond the size of your fist?

_____

Who in your house could you trust to help you hide that diamond?

_____

What would you say to the gang of international jewel thieves who show up at your door after you double-crossed them to keep the diamond for yourself?

_____

_____

Does your house have a beef jerky room? If yes, how big? *If not, do better.*

_____

_____

On an average day with my kids, I say these words way more often than I'm comfortable with.

Find them in the word search below.

LOUD	MISSING	ELECTRIFIED
STICKY	CLOGGED	COMBUSTIBLE
SUSPICIOUS	SHATTERED	CURSED

```
C O M B U S T I B L E D C M Z
D E I F I R T C E L E E U K J
E M I S S I N G N B T G R O F
S U S P I C I O U S Z G S I L
J L F Y B E B O W X K O E X S
W I E C H M R G K V Q L D J H
D E R E T T A H S Y K C I T S
```

Make a sentence out of all those words. *Plus any extras you need to make it a complete thought.*

_____

_____

_____

Congratulations, you have an accurate summary of my day. Now I need to sit down. *Did your day sound like that? If so, maybe take it easy on your parents tomorrow.*

Here are some more posts about my kids.

7-year-old: When I have a mansion, you can visit.

Me: Awww.

7: So you can clean it.

7-year-old: My book is broken.

Me: What's wrong with it?

7: The words are too big.

5-year-old: *crisis wail* My shoes are too small.

Me: You grew.

5: My shoes should grow, too.

Write some posts of your own.

Chuckle, Don't Choke

Actually, I can. It's 9,738, but who's counting?

Everybody eats. I can't tell you how many times my kids and I have squabbled over food. I want my kids to eat healthy food. They want to eat literally anything else. The battle never ends.

> **7-year-old:** *looks sadly at her green beans*
>
> **Me:** What's wrong with them?
>
> **7:** They're not pizza.

What's a food other people like but you would never ever eat, even if it meant you'd starve?

What did that food do to you to make you hate it so much? *If it never wronged you, make something up.*

If you are an evil genius, be yourself.

Imagine you're an evil genius. Write down a scheme to rid the world of your least favorite food once and for all. Let's be honest: Those carrots had it coming.

It's hard to appreciate the humor around you on an empty stomach.

Connect the descriptions on the left to the foods on the right to create a snack as unique as you.

DESCRIPTIONS	FOODS
Chocolate-covered	Pancakes
Pickled	Bratwurst
Spicy	Taffy
Vegetarian	Slugs
Deep-fried	Bowl of salt
Salted	Void
Incinerated	Cookies
Interdimensional	Ice cream

What's your ultimate snack that helps you stay creative? *It doesn't have to be on the list.*

_____

_____

_____

_____

_____

_____

_____

_____

My kids are picky eaters. Maybe you are, too. That's okay. There was a time when I didn't like many foods, either.

Here's what my kids think of different foods:

- **Cheese:** An appropriate topping for everything, including other toppings
- **Chocolate milk:** Nectar of the gods
- **Potatoes:** As fries, good. As mashed potatoes, a mouthful of disappointment

How would you describe these foods?

- **Meat loaf** _____
  _____
  _____
  _____

- **Brussels sprouts** _____
  _____
  _____
  _____

- **Nachos** _____
  _____
  _____
  _____

- **An ice sculpture of a swan** _____
  _____
  _____
  _____

It's food if you can lick it, right?

As well as a few I added using their logic.

These are some terms my kids have used for different foods. Thinking like them, match up the real food with the kid-centric name for it.

Real Name	Better Name
1. Parmesan cheese	A. Cow juice
2. Bagel	B. Cry apples
3. Lasagna	C. Sad doughnut
4. Milk	D. Baby cookies
5. Cookie dough	E. Spaghetti sprinkles
6. Onions	F. Noodle cake

Now draw one of those foods the way my kids describe it.

It's easier to laugh on a full stomach. I mean, not physically. There's a lot of food sloshing around in there. Everything just seems funnier when you're not hangry.

Cracked Up by the Bell

There's no place where more things can go wrong than a school cafeteria.

Here are some possible disasters.

- You solve the mystery of the mystery meat, but you wish you hadn't.
- You spill ketchup on your shirt and now people think you're a sloppy vampire.
- The lunch lady continues giving you daily updates on her bunions.
- Someone stole your lunch and now the thief is mad at you because you used the wrong kind of cheese.

Now you list some.

- _____
  _____
- _____
  _____
- _____
  _____
- _____
  _____
- _____
  _____

Everybody has a least favorite day. For most of us, it's the first day of the school week. Here's what my kids think of **The Day That Shall Not Be Named**.

4-year-old: Is it Friday?

Me: No, it's Monday.

4: *flops on the floor*

Apparently it's too early for bad news.

Me: Wake up.

7-year-old: Is it a stay-at-home day?

Me: No, it's a school day.

7: Wake me up when it's not.

Write your own conversation about how you want to avoid your least favorite day of the week.

Don't wait till you get home to have fun. Find laughter at school. Just do it quietly. *This book doesn't count as a valid excuse to get out of detention.*

Reasons to find the humor in traveling:

- It makes the trip seem shorter.
- It gives you something to do if you're not sleeping.
- It stops you from abandoning annoying family members at the next rest stop.

Some of my favorite posts are from when we were on the road:

packing luggage for all four kids
Me: Will all this fit in the van?
Wife: If we don't take the kids.
Me: Consider it done.

at the gas station
Me: Do you need to go potty?
5-year-old: No.
Me: Are you sure?
5: Uh-huh.

Me: Are you absolutely positive?
5: YES.
Me: *pulls back onto the road*
5: I have to pee.

Write a post about something annoying that a family member did the last time you were traveling together.

_____

_____

Does it seem less annoying now? Of course not. At least you got a joke out of it.

Staying away from home is always dangerous because you're in a place you don't own. That means when you break something, you have to replace it. *Or hide the evidence.*

> ***shattering sound in the next room***
> **Me:** What was that?!
> **7-year-old:** Everything staying in one piece.
> **Me:** Sounds legit.

If you broke something, what would you do?

1. Admit it.
2. Replace it and hope no one notices.
3. Hide it.
4. Change your name and flee the country.
5. Reassemble it with magic.

Why?

_____
_____
_____
_____
_____
_____
_____
_____
_____

There are no wrong answers.
Actually, I'm pretty sure number three is wrong. And number five isn't really an option unless you got your letter from Hogwarts.
(Check for owls just in case.)

Road trips are never easy with my kids.

Draw upgrades to this minivan to make my trip easier.

A few suggestions

- A snowplow blade to push aside snow and/or zombies
- Helicopter rotors
- Invisible cloak (just color the page white)

My kids love camping. And by "camping," I mean putting sleeping bags on the floor of their bedroom and watching videos till they fall asleep. *Things can get pretty rugged in my house.*

Picture your ideal campsite. What would it have?

_____

_____

_____

What wouldn't it have?

_____

_____

_____

How would you defend against Bigfoot?

_____

_____

_____

What's the most impressive object you'd use to smash a mosquito? *Mine's a participation trophy.*

_____

_____

_____

Wherever you go, always pack your sense of humor. And your toothbrush. Nobody wants to hear your jokes if your breath stinks.

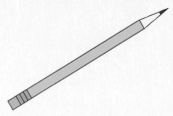

Art Attack

A comic is just a back-and-forth conversation with pictures. Anyone can draw one. Don't believe me? I've made THOUSANDS of comics, and the last time I tried to draw a dog, it looked like an angry pineapple.

Including a bunch that were published in a book.

Draw characters to go with the dialogue below.

> Character 1: Do you hear that? It's my favorite
>
> sound in the whole world.
>
> Character 2: What?
>
> Character 1: My voice.
>
> Character 2: My favorite sound is when it stops.

You can draw people, animals, inanimate objects, or nothing at all.

Invisible people have conversations, too.

There's no wrong way to draw. Unless you draw evil symbols that summon a monster that destroys the world.

Draw two people talking to each other. They can be as simple or elaborate as you want.

And even then, that's the right way if you're an evil wizard or angsty artist.

Try not to summon that world-destroying monster, but if you do, no hard feelings. You do you.

Now give them some dialogue. Here's the first line:

Do you know how to draw a comic?

Take it from there.

Grrr

Every day, I take some of my kids' drawings and turn them into comics. But sometimes my kids don't draw two people (or animals, plants, etc.) who can talk to each other. How do I get around that? I draw word balloons leading to the edge of the comic like two people are talking to each other from just out of the frame.

Draw something completely random in the boxes below.

Now add the word balloons like two people are having a conversation about whatever you drew. Or leave the panels blank and write a conversation about that. You can be as elaborate (or lazy) as you want.

Unicorns Have a Point

When I started writing jokes, I called my website Exploding Unicorn. The name is based on a fake book of the Bible I wrote back when I was in high school. *I'm really old.*

Here are some unicorn facts you might not know:

- All unicorns have the middle name Steve.
- Unicorns have corks on the tip of their horns before they're born so they don't jab their moms on the way out.
- Unicorns are magical, but their only magic is card tricks. They don't do them very often because they don't have thumbs.

Write your own unicorn facts. No one has ever seen a real one, so you can't be wrong.

- _____
  _____
- _____
  _____
- _____
  _____
- _____
  _____

Here's a completely true, scientifically accurate encyclopedia entry about unicorns—but it's missing some words.

Fill in the blanks. Warning: What you put here will become a permanent part of unicorn lore. No pressure.

www.unicornorpegasus.org/Unicorns

For other uses, see Unicorn (exploding).

Contrary to popular belief, unicorns mostly live in _____.
(country)
They sleep _____ hours a day, and only wake up when
(number between 1 and 24)
they're feeling _____. Their diet consists almost entirely
(feeling)
of _____, which they eat covered in _____. They need to
(plural noun)   (topping)
eat at least _____ of them a day to stay alive.
(number)

Unicorns never _____. They find it to be
(verb)
_____. Instead, they prefer to _____,
(adjective)   (verb)
which they do while wearing _____.
(article of clothing)
But clothed unicorns never show up in art because
their outfits offend _____, who prefers
(celebrity)
to see unicorns in the nude. Although unicorns
seem to resemble horses, their closest animal
relative is actually the _____. They still
(animal)
sometimes see each other at family reunions. They
both find the encounters to be _____.
(adjective)

Unicorns

Not pictured: His popped balloon.

Group	Magical Horse Thingies
Similar creatures	Pegasus, Zebra with spikes
Mythology	Everywhere but Canada (Don't ask)
Other names	Pointy Pony, Stabby Horse Guy

People often mix up unicorns and Pegasi (which is the plural of "Pegasus," I have decided). Here are the similarities and differences.

	UNICORNS	PEGASI
Most common color:	White	White
Number of legs:	Four	Four
Number of appendixes:	One	Zero (had it removed in grade school)
Horn:	Yes	No
Wings:	No	Yes
Good at texting:	Yes	Unknown
Looks good in flannel:	Yes	Yes
Mime skills:	Decent	Subpar

So there you have it. If you ever see an unidentified horselike creature, ask it to pretend it's trapped in an invisible box. Then you'll know what it is.

Remember, unicorns are outdoor pets. You do NOT want them exploding inside. Your room is messy enough as it is.

Zombie Dodging

For fun, my kids and I train to fight zombies. Zombies aren't real, but it's an excuse to exercise, and it makes our neighbors nervous. *Always a plus.*

yet

Here are some fun activities you can do by yourself or with others to get ready for the zombie apocalypse:

- Time how long it takes you to lock all your doors and windows. *This is also a great defense against door-to-door salespeople.*
- Practice fighting with a broom. It'll make you great at defeating zombies. *And dust bunnies.*
- Stockpile food near your bed. It will be a lifesaver if you get trapped in your room by zombies or if you just want a snack in the middle of the night.

What other activities can you think of that could double as zombie training?

- _____
- _____
- _____
- _____

73

Can you spot the differences between these two pictures? *It's subtle.*

Color in both pictures.

You're about to take a bite of the best sandwich you've ever made when a zombie comes after you. They're jerks like that.

Draw a comic about what you do next.

It's important to have an escape path in the event of a zombie attack. Here's mine. I'd save my wife and kids and then my pigs and dog. Somewhere in there, I'd grab the microwave, too.

There's no point in surviving the apocalypse if I can't microwave frozen burritos.

Front porch

Garden hose

Betsy

Mae

Me

Lucy

Lola

Waffle

Ark of the Covenant

Luna

Microwave

Gilly

Niko

Snacks

Here be dragons

Meaning of Life

Junk I should have cleaned up months ago

Safety

Now draw the floor plan of your house and mark the best escape path in the event of a zombie attack.

Be sure to account for any family members or supplies you want to save.

77

A unicorn meets a zombie. Do they fight? Do they become friends? Do they fall in love?

Draw the results below.

Nobody knows exactly what will happen in the zombie apocalypse.

Fill in this intelligence report to let people know what zombies are really like.

Everybody thinks zombies are scary. But actually, they're
_____. It's easy to stop them if you have a
    (adjective)
_____. Just _____ with it. You know what
    (noun)   (verb)
I'm talking about.

A group of zombies is called a _____. You're
                                      (noun)
most likely to spot them in _____. They like
                                  (city)
hanging out there because of all the _____.
                                          (plural noun)
If you see a group of zombies approaching, the first thing
you should do is _____. Do it _____.
                      (verb)   (adverb)
I'm not kidding.

Whatever you do, don't _____. That's a sure way to
                            (verb)
end up _____. Follow these tips and you should be
          (adjective)
_____. Good luck.
    (adjective)

Fill in this table for the differences between undead zombies and living people.

	UNDEAD ZOMBIES	LIVING PEOPLE
Speed:		
Amount of air they need to breathe:		
Likelihood of a limb randomly falling off in the middle of the day:		
Ease of finding others with similar interests to hang out with:		
Number of outfits they own:		
Diet:		
Amount they complain:		

Defeating zombies is easy if you have the right tools.

Solve this crossword puzzle full of everyday household items that are also awesome zombie-slaying weapons.

DOWN

1. Old home movie player that's heavy enough to topple a zombie if you toss it at them

2. Unclogs toilets or suctions zombies' faces off

5. Foam projectile that can hit a zombie right in the eye

7. Portable computer or mobile zombie face-smasher

ACROSS

3. Two-wheeled, human-powered zombie-evasion vehicle

4. Vehicle with sliding doors perfect for carpooling or escaping zombies

6. Four-wheeled device for pushing babies and whacking zombies

8. Building blocks that neither zombies nor humans can bear to step on

Today's Setups, Tomorrow's Punch Lines

Where do you see yourself in five years?

How do you see yourself there? *Seriously, do you have special time-travel eyes that let you peer into the future?*

Is there anything you can tell me about the future that we can use to make money now? Winning lottery numbers would be great.

~~**What's your favorite color?**~~ *Let's get back to that moneymaking thing. Future secrets. **Spill them now.***

What's your favorite food? *Will that food still exist in the future (or should I buy a whole bunch of it and hide it in my basement)?*

Thanks to the internet, you can share the things you find funny with people around the world. But if you want to go all over the world yourself, it's not as convenient.

Draw a map of the world so it suits you. Label your favorite places.

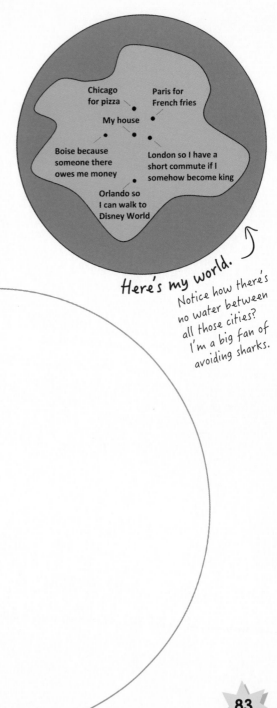

Chicago for pizza

Paris for French fries

My house

Boise because someone there owes me money

London so I have a short commute if I somehow become king

Orlando so I can walk to Disney World

Here's my world.

Notice how there's no water between all those cities? I'm a big fan of avoiding sharks.

It's easy to find the humor in ordinary situations. But what about extraordinary ones? Let's say you got sucked into your favorite movie and now you have to live it out.

What movie are you in?

_____

Which character are you?

_____

Who would you want to take with you?

_____

_____

Could you solve the problems better than your favorite characters?

_____

_____

What would you tell your parents when you got back?

_____

_____

Would you want to be in the sequel? _Assuming you survived the first movie and the money is right._

_____

_____

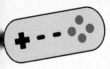

Another boring day?
Reimagine your life as a video game.

Who is the final boss?

_____

_____

What do you eat for a power-up?

_____

_____

What do you collect for bonus points?

_____

_____

Who are the common enemies you see on every level?

_____

_____

How do you defeat them?

_____

_____

What song plays if you beat a level?

_____

_____

What song plays if you lose?

_____

_____

_____

_____

Everyone needs a nickname. Sadly, people in real life never call me Exploding Unicorn to my face. I guess I haven't earned it.

What's a nickname you wish you could earn?

In your dream scenario, how would you earn it?

What's one nickname you never want?

How can you avoid it?

What do you think your catchphrase is?

What do your friends think your catchphrase is?

What do your parents think your catchphrase is?

What does your pet think your catchphrase is?

If you still can't think of a catchphrase, write down the first thing you say when you get to school every day. You can make it up. This book is entirely fact-free.

We're almost out of pages so I have to leave you.

Congratulations, Comedy Ninja

If you can find the humor in
unfair teachers, flaky friends, and undead
monsters walking the earth, you can laugh at
anything. You're ready to take on the world.
The world won't know what hit it. Seriously,
bend down and start punching the ground.
The world will have no idea.

Go forth and laugh often. Love much.
Survive always. And keep an eye out for
unicorns. They're out there. You just have to
believe—and have a good net.
It's the only way to catch them.

Let's explore how you've changed since the start of this journal.

Before this book, I was _____. Now I'm _____.
(adjective)   (adjective)

These changes make me feel _____. Deep down, I
(adjective)

know the only one who can change me is _____,
(person's name)

but I haven't seen them in a while. Maybe they're hiding in

my _____.
(a room)

Most importantly, I know this book was _____.
(adjective)

I'm very _____ that I won't sue James Breakwell.
(feeling)

I _____ absolve him of liability. This statement is
(adverb)

legally _____.
(adjective ending in "ing")

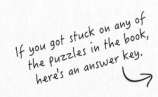

If you got stuck on any of
the puzzles in the book,
here's an answer key.

88

Answer key:

page 8

page 60

Parmesan cheese = Spaghetti sprinkles

Bagel = Sad doughnut

Lasagna = Noodle cake

Milk = Cow juice

Cookie dough = Baby cookies

Onions = Cry apples

page 15

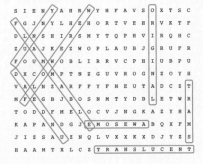

page 74

If you didn't get this one, see a doctor. You are becoming a zombie.

page 50

page 81

page 55

A Short Goodbye

Hopefully you've made important discoveries about yourself and recorded lots of great memories. And maybe you even learned how to fly. Not from me, of course. I was too busy, as promised. But there's nothing to stop you from doing some research on your own. Take some initiative. I can't do everything for you. But while I can't protect you from gravity, I can keep sharing my life on the internet. If you're curious about what I'm up to, ask your parents to find me here:

Twitter: @XplodingUnicorn

Facebook: www.facebook.com/ExplodingUnicorn

Instagram: @james_breakwell

YouTube: www.youtube.com/jamesbreakwell